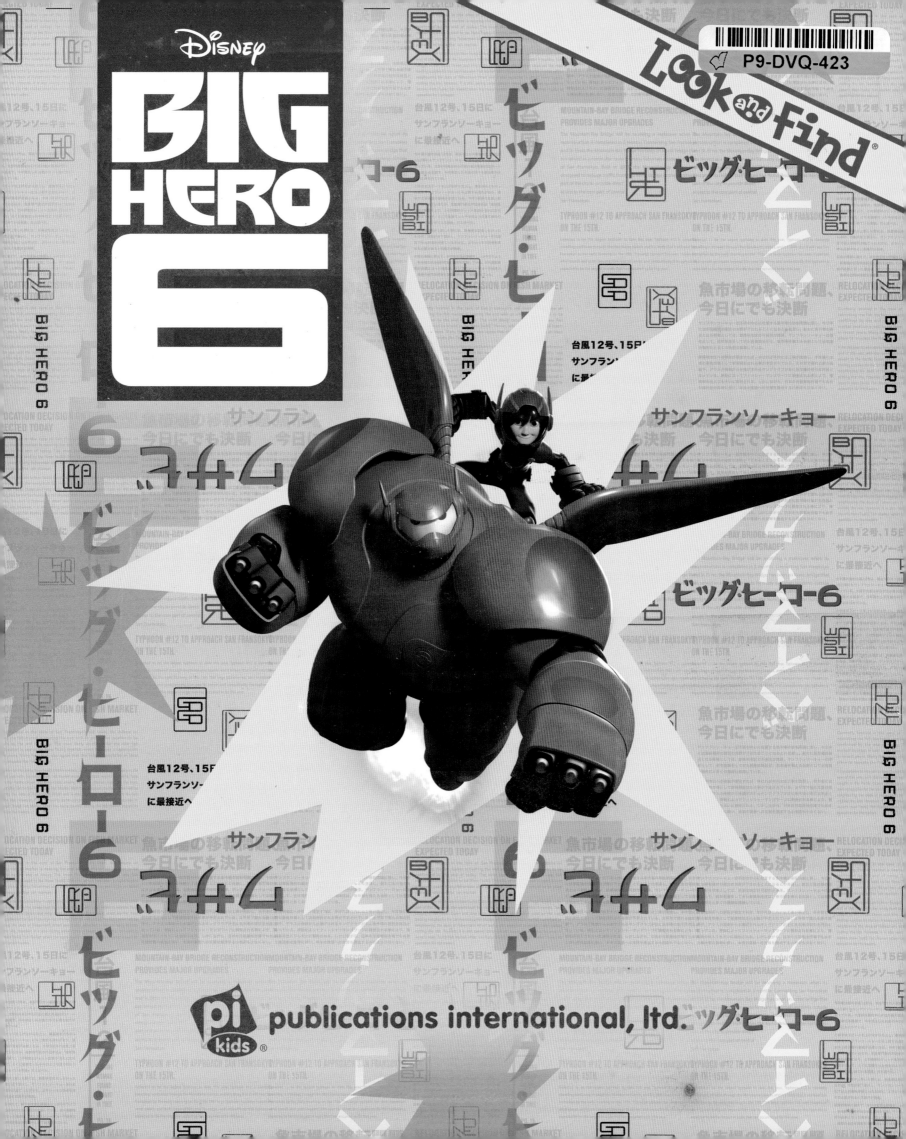

Disney

BIG HERO 6

Look and Find®

pi kids

publications international, ltd.

When your best friends are all brilliant inventors, most of your time is spent working on projects. As everyone tinkers away, look around for Hiro and his brother Tadashi, and their creative friends:

Hiro

Tadashi

Wasabi

Go Go

Honey

Fred

It's time for the Tech Showcase! Hiro shows off his invention—tiny robots that are controlled by his thoughts via a headband to form any shape or carry any object. The crowd loves them! As Professor Callaghan tells Hiro he has been admitted to San Fransokyo Institute of Technology, find microbots in these shapes:

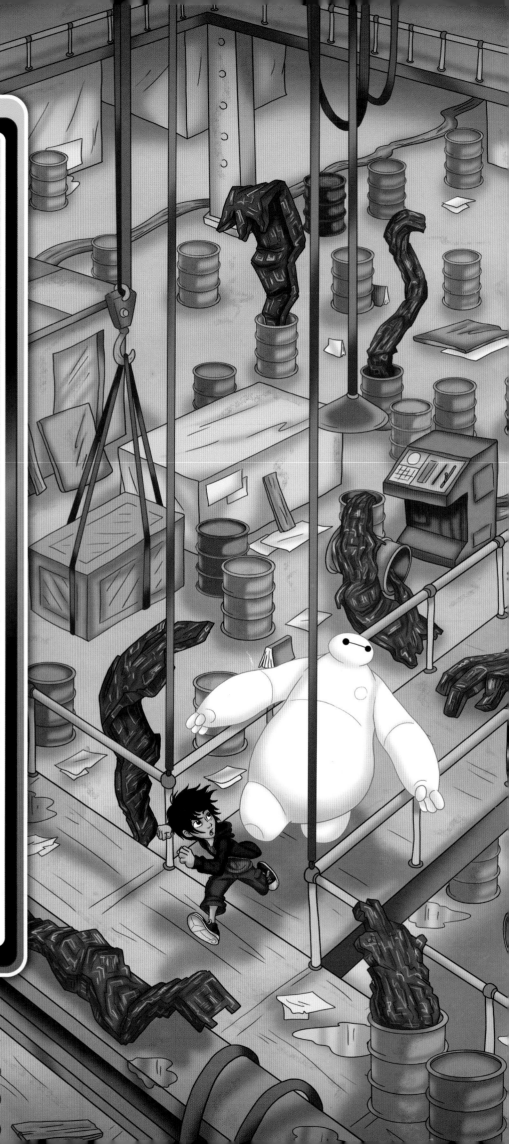

After the showcase, a fire destroys Hiro's microbots, and Professor Callaghan and Tadashi are unable to escape. All Hiro has left to remind him of his brother is Baymax, Tadashi's personal healthcare companion robot. Then one day, Hiro finds a microbot under his bed. It leads Hiro and Baymax to a warehouse filled with TONS of microbots! A mysterious masked man named Yokai is controlling them. Can you find Yokai and these microbots?

Hiro and Baymax try to reclaim Hiro's microbots, but Yokai immediately sends the bots after them. Just then, a car pulls up. Wasabi, Fred, Honey, and Go Go have come to the rescue! As Yokai chases Hiro and his friends through the streets of San Fransokyo, search for these things in the chaos:

this store sign

Yokai

this sidewalk sign

Baymax

this plant

this shipping container

At Fred's house (really a mansion!) Hiro tells his friends that he is sure Yokai stole his microbots and set the fire at the showcase. Hiro and Baymax need all the help they can get to defeat Yokai. And so, Big Hero 6 is born! As everyone suits up, look around for these team members and their new high-tech super powers:

Baymax's rocket fist

Hiro

Fred's fire

Honey's chem-balls

Wasabi's laser hands

Go Go's super skates

Baymax's super sensor locates Yokai on Akuma Island. There, the heroes find a lab full of video monitors, which show a failed experiment involving teleportation portals, a woman named Abigail, and a familiar looking man. Hiro thinks the man in the video is Yokai. Can you find the real Yokai, plus these video images?

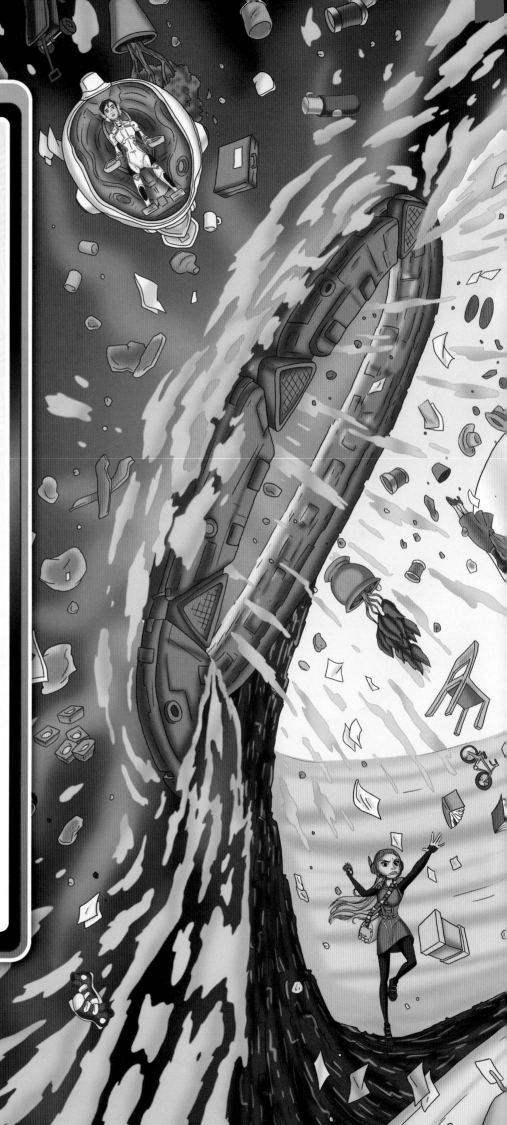

It turns out that Yokai is… Professor Callaghan! And Abigail is Callaghan's daughter. Callaghan set the fire at the showcase so he could steal Hiro's microbots and get revenge! In town, Callaghan reassembles the portal and activates it. As anything and everything gets sucked into the portal, find the six heroes who come to the rescue, plus the surprise save that Baymax makes:

Hiro & Baymax

Fred

Honey

Go Go

Wasabi

Abigail

Big Hero 6 did it! They saved the city, and Abigail! As the news crew does their report on the "mystery people" who came to the rescue, search for these students on campus:

Hiro

Wasabi

Honey

Fred

Go Go

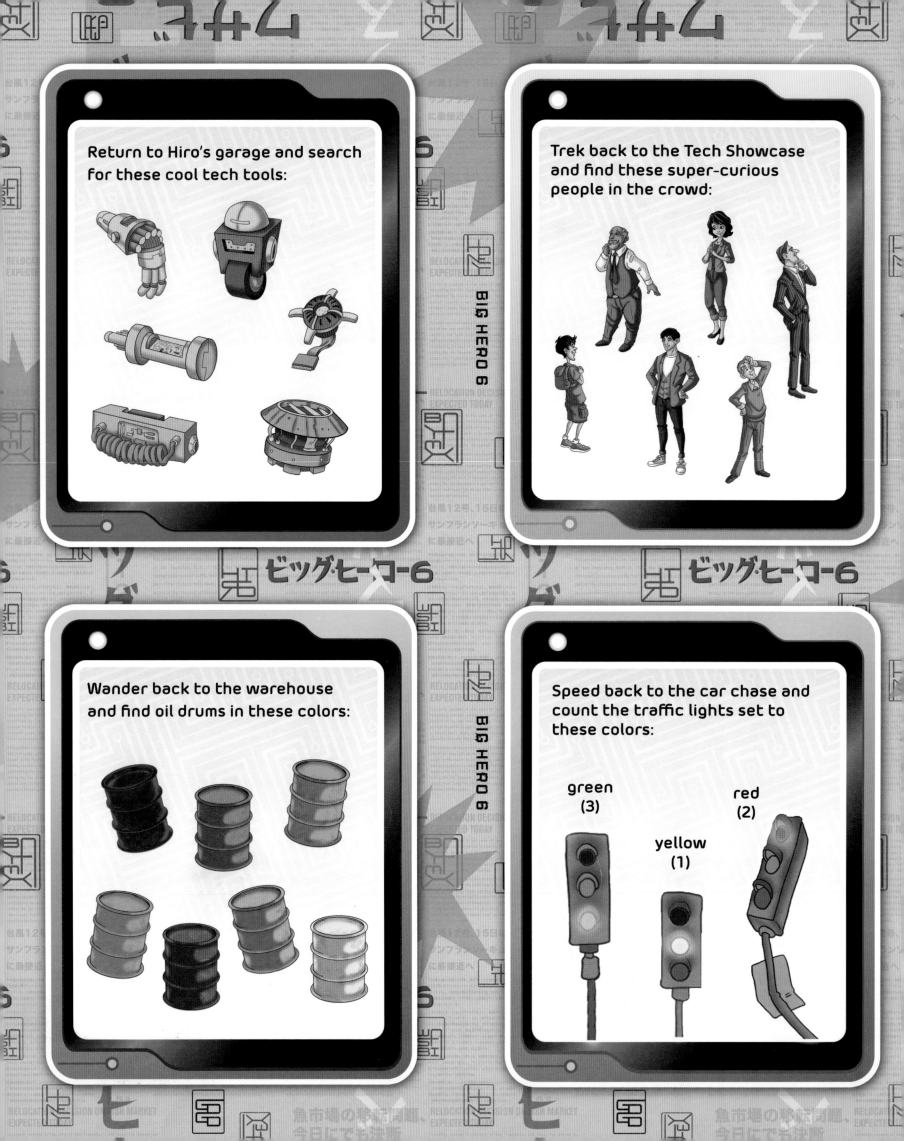

Return to Hiro's garage and search for these cool tech tools:

Trek back to the Tech Showcase and find these super-curious people in the crowd:

Wander back to the warehouse and find oil drums in these colors:

Speed back to the car chase and count the traffic lights set to these colors:

green
(3)

yellow
(1)

red
(2)

ビッグ・ヒーロー6

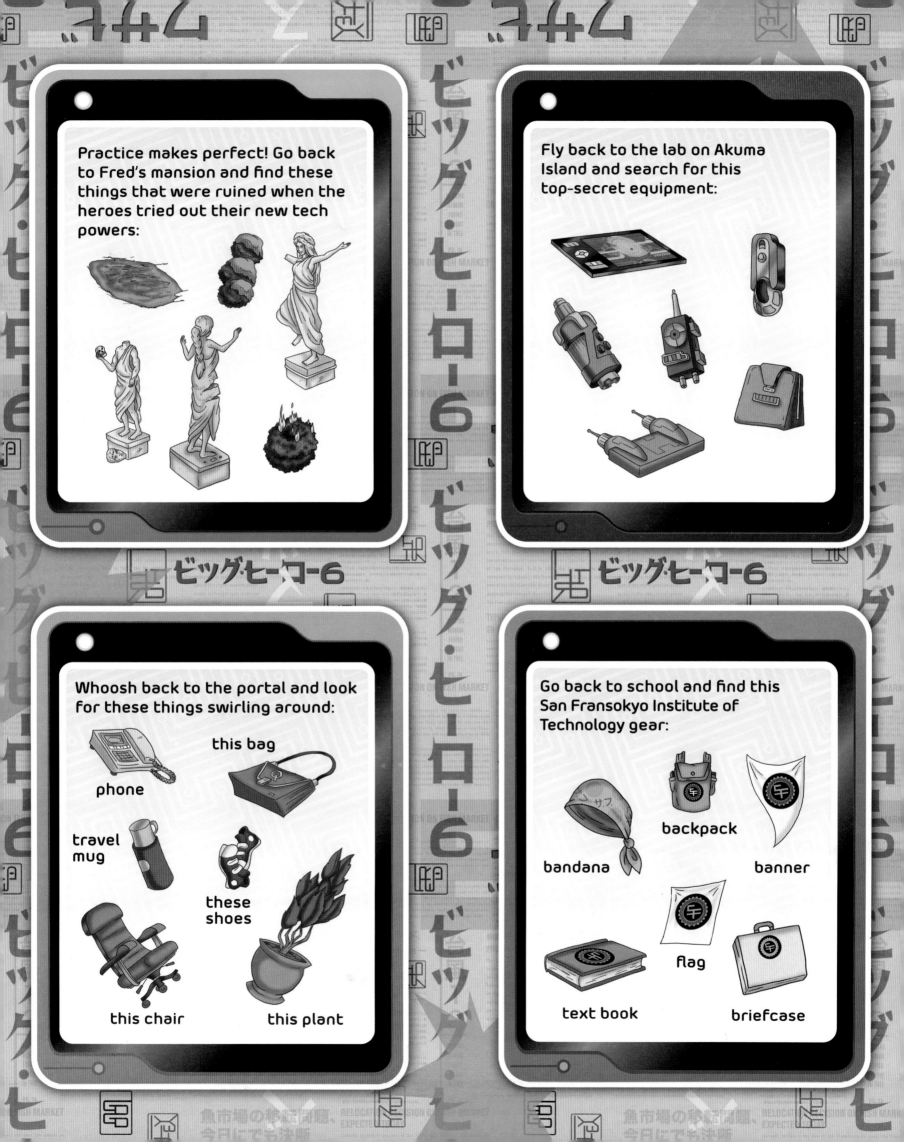

Practice makes perfect! Go back to Fred's mansion and find these things that were ruined when the heroes tried out their new tech powers:

Fly back to the lab on Akuma Island and search for this top-secret equipment:

Whoosh back to the portal and look for these things swirling around:

phone

this bag

travel mug

these shoes

this chair

this plant

Go back to school and find this San Fransokyo Institute of Technology gear:

bandana

backpack

banner

flag

text book

briefcase